Hospice
for Our
Furry Friends

By
PAULETTE LEWIS-BROWN

authorHOUSE®

AuthorHouse™
1663 Liberty Drive
Bloomington, IN 47403
www.authorhouse.com
Phone: 1 (800) 839-8640

Published by AuthorHouse 11/19/2018

ISBN: 978-1-5462-6726-3 (sc)
ISBN: 978-1-5462-6725-6 (e)

Print information available on the last page.

This book is printed on acid-free paper.

Contents

WHEN I LOST MY DOG MOLLY.
JESUS SAID MY DEAR YOU WILL
BE STRONG ENOUGH TO START
HOSPICE FOR OUR FURRY FRIENDS.
REACH OUT TO OTHERS LIKE YOURSELF.
LOYALTY NEVER DIES. TRUE
FRIENDS LIVES ON FOREVER.
EVEN IN OUR DREAMS.

A Good Life

You Gave Me A Good Life
Please Don't Blame Yourself
Time Has Come For Me To Go
Home To Be With Someone Else.
The Creator Of The Universe
Knows My Name. You Were The
Best Mom And Dad, Forever Will
Stay. October 17th I Took My
Last Breath, You Stood By My
Bedside And Comfort My Fears.
Tears Flows Without A Pause.
Then One Final Note Came In.
Let Go My Dear You Gave Molly
A Very Good Life. Max Is On The
Other Side Waiting For Her To
Come Home. Rub Her Paws
Tickle Or Ears, Kiss Her Nose.
Nothing To Fear . You
Were There Until The End.
Forever Best Friends.

Lost Puppy

I Feel Like A Lost Puppy
Without You.

Where's My Walking Buddy
Where's My Side Kick

Where Is My Little Furry Friend
When I Feel Sick.
When Will See Her Waggly Tail.

When Will I Ever Feel Happy Again.
Tell Me What To Do.
I Feel Like A Lost Puppy
Without You.

Help Me Lord
To Find My Way Home.

One Angel Note

Think Of Me
When The Sun ☀
Shines.
Think Of Me
When It Rains.
Think Of Me
When The Birds
Sings. Every
Thought Will
Give You Wings.
Smile When You
Think Of Me.
This Is One Angel
Note.
Passed It Around.
Please Think Of Me.
When Times Get Rough
My Memories Will Carry
You Through

Molly

My Heart Collapsed
Rubbing Your Paws
I Am Going To Feel Like
A Lost Doggy From Mars
No More Waggly Tail.
My Eyes Are Weak,Frail And
Flooding In Tears.
Where Is My Furry Friend
Molly Dear.
Lord Please Step In To
Comfort My Soul.
Help Me To Let Go Of
Molly Toys.Few More Days.
Just To Say Good Bye
I Wanna Be Strong But
Why I Feel So Weak And Sad.
This Moment Is For My
Molly . Forever Loved.
Oh Help Me God.

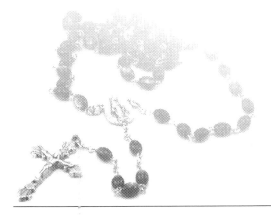

My Love Lives On

My Love Lives On Forever
Don't Shed Anymore Tears .
I Am With You Always My Dear.
Read This Poem Underneath
A Palm Tree, Watch It Sways.
Start Hospice For Your Furry Friends
Be Very Brave.
Time To Make New Friends
With The Same Interest.
Think Of Me Daily
Until Eternity Rest.
My Love Lives On.
Forever Your Very Best Friend.
Move Forward Is Your Clue.
I Love You.

Where Were You

Father God
Where Were You
When Molly Took Sick
Where Were You When
My Heart Feel Like A
Brick. Where Were You
When I Crawl Under The
Table, Just To Lay Down With Molly.
I Already Know The Answer.
Father God You Were Right There With Me.
This I Know.
You Were Keeping Me Strong
For Doggy Molly To Glow.
Thank You Lord For This Moment
To Clear My Mind.
You Will Forever Be My Best Friend.

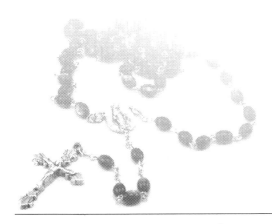

First Time Without You.

This's My First Thanksgiving
Without You.
This's Going To Be My First
Christmas Too.
I Already Have An Agenda
Of Things To Do.
I Will Water The Flowers
By Your Grave Site.
I Will Wait For The Sun ☀ To Rise.
I Will Give Thanks 🙏
For Every Year
That I Was Blessed With You.
My First Time Will Not Be Easy,
But Father God Will See Me Through.
This's Going To Be My First Valentines
Without You Too.
But I Will Always Love You❤🐾.
Forever So Kind.

Walk with me

Walk with me on this journey.
Please hold my hands.
Feel my positive energy
Create a new bond.
Let go of the pain inside.
Our pain will be at different levels.
Balance
Life journey embracing each other.
Our furry friends
are waggling their tails.
Wearing their loyalty dress 👗.
Look at all the Males clapping 🖐🖐.
Just walk with me.
Feel blessed.
Walk With Me My Queen.

Flower Bed

Make Me A Flower Bed
Call My Name.

Make Me A Name Sake To
Rest My Head.

Create Your Own Happiness
Build A Peace Of Mind

In The Future Every Animal
Will Have A Shelter To Call.

Molly Oh So Kind.
Make Me A Flower Bed
Forever.

Hospice

Hold My Paws

Wipe My Tears
Away.

Comfort Me In
My Despair.

At This Point
I Only Need One
Guest. Sitting On
My Chair.

Hospice For Our
Furry Friends.
This Is Your First
Clue .
Every Home Needs
One. Pink Or Blue.

Here's A Comfort Case
Package For You.

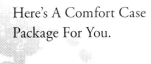

It's Okay To Mourn

Its Okay To Mourn
Don't Feel Restricted
When You're Mourning
The Loss Of Your Furry
Friends . I Do Understand
I Went Down This Road
Too. Moment Of Silence
To Gather Up Memories.
Prayer For Everyone In
This Room.
It's Okay To Feel Blue
So Molly Wants Me To
Give This Pink Gift 💔 To
You.
It's Okay To Mourn For The
Chosen Few.
Life Is Filled With
Many Avenues
It's Okay To Mourn.

Join Me

Join Me To Celebrate
This Mission Molly Day.
Its A Very Special Day
October 17th.
Pray For Every Furry
Friend Who Is Going
Through A Hard Time
Letting Go. Uplift Their
Owners With Love.
On This Day I Will Celebrate
Hospice For Our Furry Friends.
Join Me In Holding Hands And Paws
Until The End.

Take Care Of My Family

Take Care Of My Earth
Angel Family For Me.
I Am On My Way
To Doggy Heaven Soon.
Where All The Other Animals
Are Waiting For Me.
Cry No More, Sing Or Read
A Special Poem For Me.
Life Without Molly And
A Touch Of True Love Lives
On, Feel Free.
Take Care Of My Adopted Family.
I Was Their True Friend.
Read This Poem Over Again.
Share With Every Family
Around The Bend.
Walking Buddy Needed.

Meow

Meow
Meow
Remember Me?
I Am On This
Journey Too
Meow
Meow 🐱
Give
My Family This
Clue. No
Matter What
No One Can
Change My Love
For Sue .
Meow 🐱
Meow 🐱
Hospice
For Me Too.
I Love You.
Meow.
Meow.

Take Me Home.

Take Me Home
Provide Comfort
Care. Include
Prescribed Medication.
Give Me Something To
Eat If I Chose To. Give Me
Water ● To The End.
Hold My Feet Rub My Paws.
Tickle My Ears.
I Have Just One ♫
More Wiggle In My Tail.
Peace And Love Forever More.
Everything Feels Better At Home.
Never Let Me Go,
Without Saying
I Love You My Little Girl.
Keep Me Home
For One More Day.
Apply One More Prayer 🙏.
Dear Lord No More Pain.
Take Me Home.
Home Sweet Home.

Molly First Tweet.

I Woke Up Feeling Blue
After Drinking My Husbands
Coffee.
I Feel Like Molly Wants Me
To Think Beyond This Note.
Don't Cry For Me My Dear
I Am Right Here By Your Bedside.
Today You Will Finish Your
9th Book, Hospice For Our Furry Friends .
Forever Loved To The End.
Tweet
Tweet.

Let Your Light Shine

Let Your Light Shine
In This Dark Time.
Bright Up The World
With Love From The Skies 🐾.
Pray For More Rain ☁️
Then Look Up To Face
The Rainbow 🌈.
Life Is Beautiful.
You're The Glow.
Smile With This Note 🎃
I Am Your Pink Bow 🎀.
Because Of You.
Everyone Knows My Name.
Your Guardian Angel 🐶
For Life.
Let Your Light Shine
Even In The Dark Times
Of Your Bark.
Smile, You're Still My Skippy Sparks ⚡
With True Love On Top .🖤📩
Be Bold And Bright.

Molly Legacy

Molly Planted Her Love On My Heart.
She Will Live Forever As Long As I Am Alive.
There Will Not Be A Day That
I Don't Think Of Molly.
Walking This Journey
I Will Never Be Alone.
In The Future Every Pet Will
Have A New Shop-Around.
Plant This Heart ♥ It Will
Grow Into A Tree 🌲 For Life.
Compliment Of Doggy Molly Legacy.
This Will Work For Everybody.
Home Sweet Home.

For Every Lonely ♥

Stand Up,
I Already Know Your Name .
Sharon, Bill And Greg.
This One Is For You.
Ralph I Know That You
Miss Me Too.
To Every Lonely Hearts 💖 ♥ 🖤.
I Love You Daily.
Send A Love Note 📧 Daily
Because I Get Lonely Too.
This's Just To Name A Few.
Peter And Pat I See You Too.
This Poem Is A Gift
For Every Lonely Hearts.
Someday True Love
Will Come Shining Through.

Hospice For Our Furry Friends

Furry Friends. This's A
Written Poem In
Golden Palm Tree.
Stop My Poems Are
Talking Open The
Poetry Gate. Walking
Poet's Tree Was
Written By Me. Poetry
Pacemaker Will
Block Any Heart
Attack. Dreams From
Beyond The Skies 🐦
More Than Any
Imagination. Jesus's
Royalty Seals The
Cake 🎂. My Author
Was A Genius Invisible
Wall. Not Everyone
Will Accept This Note.
But I Can. Hospice For
Our Furry Friends.
This Will Not Be Her
Last Book.
True Love ♥ Forever
Lives On Through Me.
Now Share Your Heart
And Order A Book
It's For A Good Cause
Hospice For Our Furry Friends

My Sugar Cane Moment.

My Jamaican Roots.
My American us Dream Will
Always Be A Paradise Of Gold.
One Doggy Memorable Note
Sends Me The Chill. Be
Strong Enough To Eat
This Sugar Cane In Memory Of Me.
Don't Forget The Papaya Tree.
Write And Feel Free.
Pass This Around And
Share Your
Sugarcane Moment.

Florida

Florida Is Beautiful
There Are Nature Everywhere
Happiness Is On Every Door.
The Sun ☀ Smiles From Over
The Fence For Sure
Everyone Is Beautiful
In A World Where People
Are So Spectacular
In Their Own Rights.
Florida Is Beautiful.
Welcome All. Every Idea 🎈
Makes Sense To One 🔔.
Show Me Your Furry Friend Art.
This's Your First
Caption Of Beautiful Florida.

Molly And Max

Two Forever Doggy Angels
Uplift Each Other While
We're Gone. Never Forget
Us In Your Beautiful Homes
You Will Forever Be In Our
Hearts. Share Memories
With Friends And Families
For A Start.
True Love From Two Doggy
Angels True Sparks, Molly
And Max Back Together
Again, In Bonded Doggy
Heaven. One Frisbee Play
Pen For All.
Molly And Max
Together Again.
Amen.

Jesus Love Animals Too

True Love Lives On Forever
Everyone Could Be Sisters
And Brothers. If We Share
Out Hearts With The World.
Love Runs Through Every
Vein. We're Not The Same In
One Frame. Masterpiece In
Every Dna. Our Furry
Friends See Loyalty This
Way. Your First Clue.
Jesus Loves Animal Too.
Thank God For Mothers
And Fathers Lucks. Trusting
Our Grandparents Books
Forever At Peace.

Bond With Nature

Bond With Nature
But Never Forget Me.
Butterflies Will Land
On Every Flowers And Trees
Even In The Winter ☃.
Every Hearts In
The World Will Always Remember
Their Furry Friends.
Especially On Valentines,
Thanksgiving And Christmas Day.
Flowers 💐 Will Put A Smile
On Your Face.
Gratitude From Every Furry Angles
Who Reads This Poem.
We're Guardian Angels Too.
Bond With Nature
For Your First Clue.
Happy Memories Will
Heal Your Souls.
Look At Every Picture And Fill
One Empty Space.
You're Never Alone
I Am With You Always.
Love Molly. ☀
Bond With Nature
But Never Forget Me.
Now Uplift Jolly.

I Want My Pwow Pwow

I Want My Pwow Pwow
Lord Help Me To See How.
I Miss My Pwow Pwow
Hmm Hmm Hmm.
Where's My Pwow Pwow
I Need My Pwow Pwow
Wuff Wuff Meow Meow
I Can't See My Pwow Pwow
Heal My Soul Dear Lord
Pwow
Pwow
I Can Feel My Pwow Pwow
My Heart Beats True Love.
Pwow
Pwow
Pwow.
I Miss You Molly.
You Were My Pwow Pwow.
Hmm
Hmm.
Puppup.
Puppup.

Kiss Everyone For Me

Hug Everyone For Me
Even The Papaya Tree.
Send A Note To Everyone
Just Remember One.
Love Everyone For Me
Someday I Will Return.
Smile With The Butterfly
That Lands On Your Skirts.
Beautiful Flowers In Every
Quarters.
Furry Friends Everywhere
For A Makeover.Beautiful
Shitzu Eyes Around The Bend.
Kiss Every Dog For Me.
Wear Your Welcome Hat
But Remember You're
Allergic To Cats.
Kiss Everyone For Me On
Every Anniversary.
October 17th A Day To
Celebrate
A Kiss From Doggy Molly.
SHITZU VALLEY.

Rainbow Bridge

Meet Me At The Rainbow Bridge.
Let's Play Frisbee Wiz
Enjoy The Bright Beauty Around.
Focus On The Eagle 🦅 Wings .
Meet Me At The Rainbow 🌈 Bridge.
Nature Will Send In The Doves 🕊 To Sing.
Every Furry Friend Will Be
Waggling Their Tails.
Read A Poem To Welcome Me Home.
On This Journey, You Will
Never Read Alone.
Meet Us At The Rainbow 🌈 Bridge.
Where Love Cuts To The Cure.
Memories Forever More.
Under The Rainbow 🌈
Bridge .
Write With A Milk Bone.
Beauty Lives On Forever More.

Empty Space

There's A Empty Space
In My Heart .
Where You Used To Be.
Your Loyalty Was My Jumpstart
One Love Will Shelter Me.
Your Paws Are Printed
Every Where I Go.
Someday I Will Smile With
The Rainbow 🌈 For A Flow.
Yesterday My Best Friend
Was Sun ☀ Shine.
The Trees Wave At Me
And Call Your Name All The Time.
Molly There's A
Empty Space In My Heart.
The Day Your Brother
Max Called You Home.
For A New Start In Doggy
Heaven.
You're Still My Best Friend
Memories Will Never End.
Empty Space Will Someday
Be Healed.

We Will Survive

We Will Survive
In My Mind You're
Still Here.
I Will Survive Sharing
Your Loyalty Gear.
Giving Comfort Care.
Spending Time With
Others Like Me.
Giving From The Heart.
And Always Feel Free.
This's A New Beginning.
Hospice For Our Furry
Friends. Give A Jumpstart
We Will Survive, Our Love
Has No Ending. It Lives
On Forever In Every Heart.
Here's Your Ribbon 🎗.
We Will Survive The Storm.
Be Calm.

Walk This Journey

Walk This Journey With me.
Soon I Will Be All Alone.
Searching The World For
Another Furry Friend
To Call My Own.
Volunteering Will Be My
First Note. Then My Faith
Will Help Me To Cope.
Walk This Journey With Me.
True Love ♥ Lives On
Every Family Tree.
October 17th.
Remember My Doggy Molly.
Walk This Journey With Me
Forever. Welcome
Mr Jolly For Acting Silly.
Smile Every Anniversary.
Then Breathe And Feel Free.
Walk This Journey With Me.

Crossroads

Meet Me At The Crossroads
Show Me The Light 💡
Keeping A Positive Attitude
Will Be Our First Sight.
Share Special Memories For
A Good Laugh.
Bonding Forever To The End
Always A Room In Every Heart ♥
For A Furry Friend.
Happiness Run 🏃‍♀️🏃 Things.
Meet Me At The Crossroads

Bond With Nature.
Jesus Loves You.
Flowers 🌼 For
Everyone In This Room.

Forever Loved.
Happy Edgar And Molly.

Molly And Max Back Together Again. IN Doggy Heaven.

Max And Molly Together Again

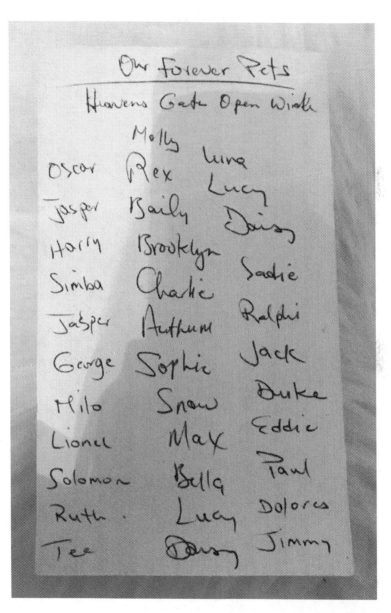

Our forever Pets

Heavens Gate Open Wide

Molly

Oscar   Rex   Nina
                 Lucy
Jasper   Baily   Daisy
Harry   Brooklyn
                  Sadie
Simba   Charlie
Jasper   Autumn   Ralph
George   Sophie   Jack
Milo   Snow   Duke
                  Eddie
Lionel   Max
                  Paul
Solomon Bella
Ruth   Lucy   Dolores
Tee   Daisy Jimmy

Hospice For Our Furry Friends. Our Legacy Lives On.

DON'T CRY FOR ME.
True Love ♥ Never Dies.

I Wish My Molly Was Here Today.
Dreams From Beyond The Skies 🎨. Bond With Nature.

My Forever Molly.

Hello Rabbits 🐰 Are Furry Too.
Give Me A Page, This's Your First Clue. Hospice For Our Furry Friends.

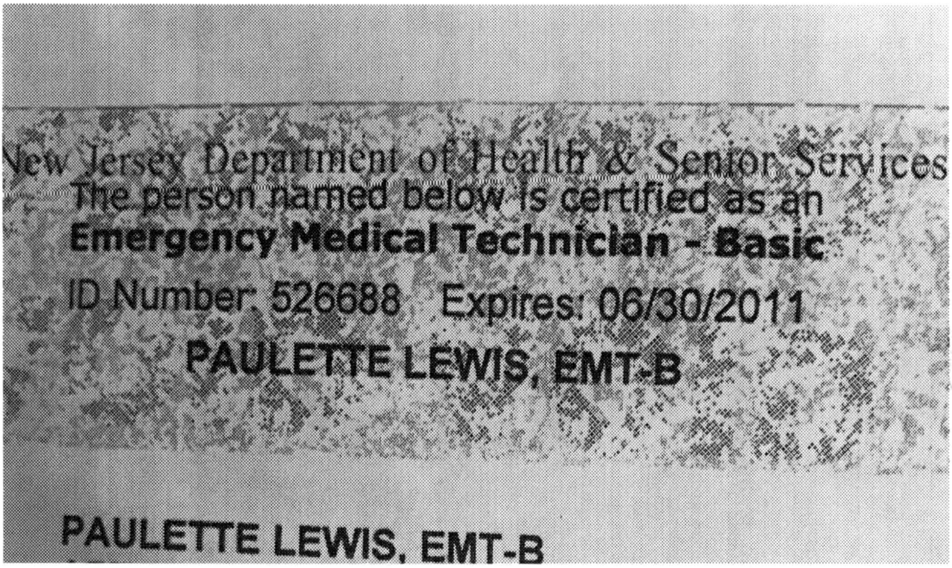

New Jersey Department of Health & Senior Services
The person named below is certified as an
Emergency Medical Technician - Basic
ID Number: 526688   Expires: 06/30/2011
PAULETTE LEWIS, EMT-B

PAULETTE LEWIS, EMT-B

FOREVER EMT

Love You Molly♥

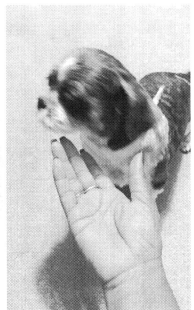

Don't Cry For Me.
True Love ♥ Never Dies.

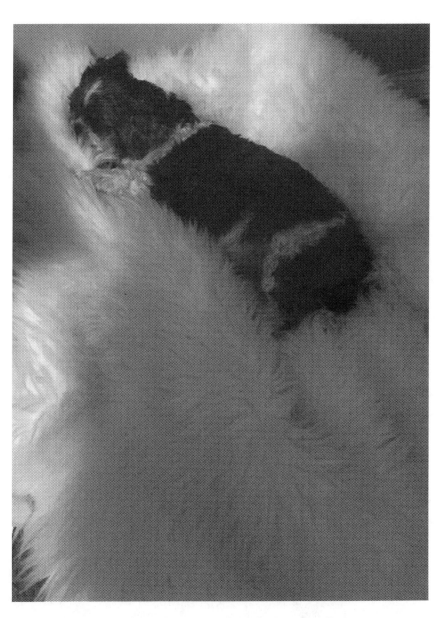

Hospice For Our Furry Friend. Comfort Care.
Will You Be There?.

To Every Hearts Focus On Uplifting Each
Other. Everyone Is On A Journey.
I Was On A Journey Too.
Hospice For Our Furry Friends. Every Animal Request.
Take This Note From One 🐾 Who Knows Best.

CHANGE MY FLOWERS EVERY SEASON.
SUNFLOWER ✹ MAKES ME SEE STARS ✦.

Smile when you see the ☀ Sun ☀
Always think of me. Beautiful Molly.

Reading Golden Palm Tree To Molly.
Poem: Hospice For Our Furry Friends.

🐾My last day with Molly 🐾

Meow
Meow
Guess ❤
My name?

Hospice for our Furry Friends.

Loyalty dances and wiggle their Tails
Their time is coming to an End.
We should care. The pain will be hard to
Bear. We will carry memories in our mental
Block, we would watch the time on our Golden
Clock. One day our Furry friend will be going
To Doggy Heaven. Give them a good life on Earth
Their love and Loyalty will always be remembered.
Hold their Paws and Tickle their Ears. Life is never
The end when we lost our Furry Friends. Pray and
Welcome Hospice for our Furry Friends.
Forever Bonded in comfort.

Golden Palm Tree.
Hospice For Our Furry Friends. Molly Approved
This Note 🐾 To The End 🦋

Smile with the Roses 🌹 in your Garden. It's okay to Kiss my Roses.

Smile With The Butterflies.
I Will Be Sending Them Your Way. 🦋

Remember The Sunflower 🌻 It Always Brightens Our Day.☀

Take care of my Chickens.
This day was all fun, fun, fun.

Molly you were my little girl.
Maybe the World will never
Understand. You will always
Be loved by one 🐾.

Molly this's my first Christmas without you.
Send me a surprise from Doggy Heaven⬚. On Christmas Day.

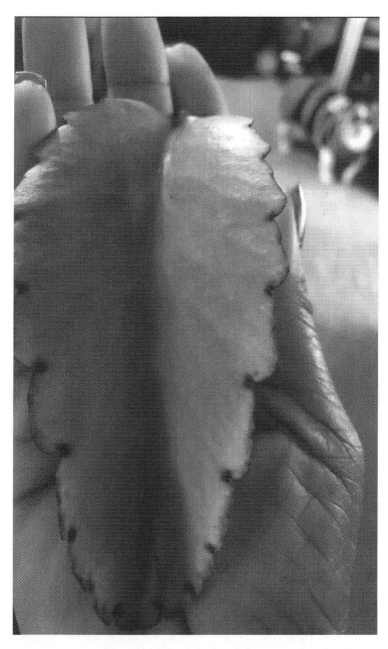

Leaf of life with Molly looking from afar.
Love you Molly. R.I.P.

Molly The Queen ♛
Forever Loved By All.

My First Christmas without you.
Merry Christmas to every lonely Hearts.
Learn to Smile again in the Rain 🌂💜✍

Welcome To My Happy Home.
My Name Is Doggy Molly.
My Mummy's Heart Is My
Permanent Home.
OCTOBER 17, 2018. Gone Too Soon.
But Will Never Be Forgotten.
♥.

Paulette Lewis

Awesome is the man
That learn to appreciate
All of Gods creation.
Green grass is a compliment of where
our economy is going.
Look up there is the beautiful blue sky.
Everything is beautiful .
My doggy Molly approve..
Awesome
By Paulette Lewis
Author/Poet

HELLO MY NAME IS MOLLY.
DO YOU REMEMBER ME?

TOMORROW WILL BE BETTER THAN TODAY.
BE STRONG FOR ONE.

WAIT A MINUTE
JUST BEFORE YOU
PUT ME DOWN TO
SLEEP.
GIVE ME ONE
SPECIAL MOMENT
WITH MY HUMAN
ANGELS FOR THE
LAST TIME.
THIS'S FOR KEEPS.
LOVE MOLLY.

Printed in the United States
By Bookmasters